Robert Kelly

The Symphonies

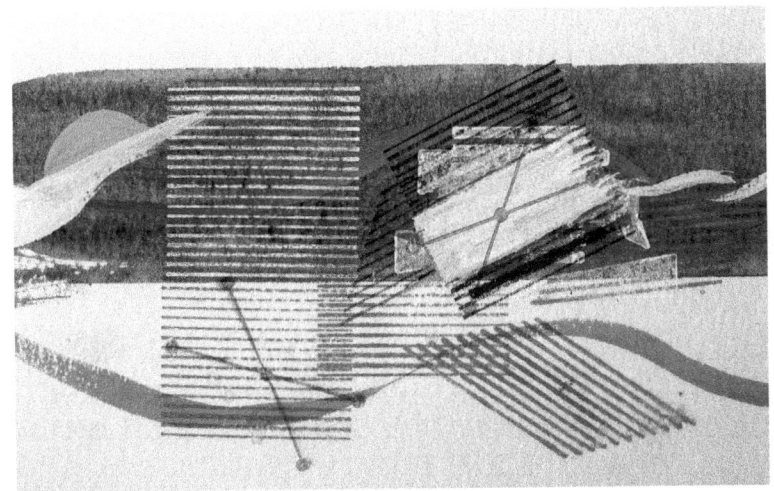

Wet Cement Press

The Symphonies ©2025
by Robert Kelly
ISBN 979-8-9918692-5-6

Library of Congress Control Number: 2025946294

Cover artwork, collage by Barbara Roether

Wet Cement Press
1908 Yolo Ave
Berkeley, CA 94707

www.wetcementpress.com

About These Symphonies

Some years ago I grew interested in the possibility of writing in direct response to music, I set out at one point then to listen to, listen through, the piano concertos of Mozart. I spent a month in winter doing just that. I enjoyed it very much—the results are a rather thickish book called *Listening Through Mozart*. A few years after that I was commissioned to do the same sort of thing with Haydn's *Seven Last Words of Christ*.

Those works and a few others like them follow this basic rule: the minute the music starts the writing must begin; the moment the music stops the writing must stop too. So that was the way which those older poems were built. Now last summer when we were on Cuttyhunk Island I suddenly began to think in quite a different way about the relationship. I'd begun to think about the possibility of a musical form developed in writing without any reference to any sound beyond the words themselves. No music in these symphonies—symphony I felt was the form I thought about because of its size, its complexity, the way in which it juxtaposes rhythms, speeds, accelerations, crescendos, tiny gestures, whispered tunes, pomp and glory, drumbeats, greatness and melancholy. I set out to write.

By the end of the summer, I had written 24 of them. Those constitute the book that I'm calling *The Symphonies*. Each one has a key signature that half-playfully suggests the mood or the aspiration of the text. Some of symphonies are small, brief. old-fashioned—think of William Boyce—or early or fully developed Haydn or even Beethoven, even Brahms weighty with striving.

All of them follow the rule of not expecting anything to be heard except as experienced through reading the language itself.

It is a desperate kind of music, writing songs without a tune in my head, trying to let words sing the truth in this anxious time.

—RK
November 2024

The Symphonies

For Charlotte,
my only island

Symphony No. 1 in C Minor

1.

The hedges across the road
were full of blue hydrangeas,
the very blue, the sort
that needs the sea, the sea
is here today, flourish of fog,
of foam, of little breezes.
It is still summer by law
but the flowers have faded,
the blue is gone. Even
the sky is pale today,
quiet and so pale. Where
did the blue go? In mind
surely we see it, what we
devote ourselves
to seeing and making seen
that persists, a while at least,
and maybe longer,
the fear swells up in me
when I see the dark green
over there unrelieved
by flowers. And free

birds, and that scares me too,
doesn't it frighten you,
the going gone of things,
the particles that hold
all this matter together,
animate it for a while
and then...and then
is it what the ages always said,
there is a soul that comes
and goes and takes a new form,
some different kind of flower?
Tumult and evening star
and maybe all those years
were right, and maybe the fog
that hides our neighbor island
hides other ways
of being too. Hope
can be more frightening than fear,
chill wind in the hedges now.

2.

Blue, I want you blue,
the way Lorca's little tune
wanted green, O you can tell
he lived in southland

mild, but we, we children,
kindle warm hopes
on our cold stone hearths,
where words sound
like other words
and quietly quietly
everything changes
but so slow you think
they must be dancing
but where is the music
they're moving to?
O blue the thought of you,
romance, more dance,
rain-dove on the balcony
and your love asleep inside.
Even midnight is a shade of blue.

3.

I want them back,
the drumroll of the obvious
shouts my demands.
What are we supposed to do
but ask and ask and get
what we can from the dark?
And when the chorus barks

How dark it is! we know
they're thinking about
their dwindling childhood,
the vanishing alertness
of growing up and seeing
one flower after another
fade away or vanish
into some aunt's vase.
No wonder the rush
through the forest,
cars hurtling through Sonora,
no wonder wonder itself
is the best tool for our research,
yes, yes, it is still summer,
hope still roars
in the cradle of the heart,
dreamy doctrines,
an afterlife made all of blue.

17 September 2024

Symphony No. 2 in G Major

1.

Sandstone came walking
up to me and said
he's the one who moves
while I and my kind
really stand still
watching the world
shape and change around us,
our bodies tremble
with reactions, we think
we're moving. But we're not.
This is serious business,
the stone said, not some silly
piping circus tune
from Disneystan, this
is the roar of space,
our only absolute,
time is just the skin
of space you notice
as it moves around you,
moves you around

and you still don't understand.
Volley of trumpets and drums.

2.

Left alone
I tried to wake,
a soft breeze
breathed through me
and I watched
what I thought
was a gate, swinging
open and closed in the wind,
a soft clean sound it made,
and it led onto a meadow.
A meadow a meadow
a parcel of heaven
I sang in the old way
a song before breakfast.
Then the stone's dark
gospel spoke in memory,
I shook it out of mind
and trotted through the gate.

3.

Or thought I did,

for surely there is grass
all round me
and a few sheep over there
and a shepherd
who looks like my father.
Or your father, so many
of us look alike, I worry,
stare away from the sheep,
sheep are nice
but not today, to say
something with more
color in it, no color no song.

4.

Then I woke some more
and stone was still talking,
that irritating calm authority
that yet is comforting too,
as if someone really knows
more than we do,
knows and would tell it
clear as a bell
over the little village
where I keep trying to be born.

18 September 2024

Symphony No. 3 in E Minor

1.

Sometimes all the finches
are so loud at morning
they chip the sunshine
and send it peeling,
reeling into sleepers
who rouse when bidden.
But not now. We wake
and wonder where
all the birds have gone,
and even so we still
contrive to hear them
loud in memory, that private
ear, feeling our way along
the long soft blue vein
that runs from yesterdays
our way, our way, our own
little now, morning anthems,
finch-frenzied, mouths of the day.

2.

Birdless breakfast,

tap the tom-tom sadly
but still we go on talking
as if it is our duty, some
bright as a rabbi reading
out loud words he knows
we know, sometimes
just on and on like a
hired hand pushing
an old-fashioned lawn mower
sluggishly back and forth
across our lawn our
lawn, our only green,
and still we hear the talk,
babble-brook and toy
piano, who are we fooling
when we speak
any word at all?
She opens her eyes
and tells me please
stop talking I'm trying
to listen to the sea.

3.

The workmen come now
to lift the river,

Minerva sent them
out of her story
into ours, slim narrative,
scarce five millennia
and who am I
even to notice such
a hasty song let alone
try to sing with it,
arrogant alto the priest
called me when I was young,
that ends my solo, now
we learn what to do
with the river, with all
the silence we've been given,
now the real stuff begins,
reality means everybody else,
the whole city you have come
all this way to hear,
louder and cleaner
all the children joying
in little pond-rich parks
and pigeons fluttering
over all that we let fall.

18 September 2024

Symphony No. 4 in A Flat

1.

Chewed gum and studied
the stars. Exactly
what he is supposed to do.
Death's magic garden
was closed today,
fog lifting, so he
is stuck with living.
Arise, he cried to Betelgeuse,
I want all the meanings, all,
to rain down on me,
little droplets of light.
And from heaven heard
a voice like his own
speaking in a language
he does not know.
Must learn. What else
Could time be for?

2.

Grammar is the first spell
to learn because it is the last

the Archons made
when they were so busy
spelling out the world.
Grammar is not too hard,
a little chewy, a taste
of wintergreen sometimes,
or elderberry in Vienna.
No, wait, geography
is another girl altogether
though she lives
in the same part of town.
Waltz with the two of them
maybe, tell all you know
and they'll tell you right back.
And what they say will be
a wreath of fragrant flowers
to wear around your neck
though it will make you
happy, dizzy, thereby often
losing your step in the dance.

3.

So dear friend, aged baby,
come home to the sky,
so much information,

so much to chew on
while your even younger kin
hurry to church and school
while you soberly estimate
the distance between
this thought and that
solitary evergreen tree
atop the little hill,
and you know
that anything we see
is out there
but we see it
in here, here,
rub your brow and
know there must be
a road between the two.
What is the road?
How far does it run?
And can we turn around
and run with it
all its other way?
Flee the cave mouth
if you see it coming–
often it looks like a kiss.

18 September 2024

Symphony No. 5 in D Minor

1.

Time to go. Time to go. Time
to go. Dress naked
for the journey,
go out now, walk
backwards, sure-
footed each step,
backwards to taste
the coming air
by what it tells
your skin, the skin
of yours you've never
seen and never will,
your secret agent
in an unknown land
who sends you messages
in her inarticulate
knowing, so you know
without knowing, go,
the wind is waiting,
keep moving, try
to be in love

with what happens,
move sure, at every
step you're already there.

2.

At the water's edge at last,
free to look out and see
so much ocean, sun swathe,
cloud, little islands
and a far coast, a boat,
a fishing boat that
for all you know
may have apostles
floating in it, coming
your way to bring
another fragment or two
of the broken word.
The sea made us
and put us here,
keep asking, keep
asking, each wave
a question. Or answer.
But how calm it is to see
even when it's raining,
it's raining now

to help us understand,
it takes a while, it takes
the whole sky to say so
but here you are.

3.

I keep saying you
but I don't know
who I do mean,
not just that I don't know
who you precisely are
or that I forget a name
I once knew, that lovely
quiet woman from Connecticut,
say, no, I mean
I may just be blithering
into the mirror, trying
to teach myself a lesson,
a lesson sleep taught me.
For I am the one
who woke up on the shore,
excited just by being,
being here. Are you
here with me?
Can you hear the waves too?

4.

Peaceful quiet of not knowing.
It's a kind of religion,
huge, ancient, rich
with ornament and statuary,
every house a vatican,
every shadow pure pageantry.
And so we know
what we can't know.
I'm singing we now
instead of you,
we're all in this together,
every subway goes there,
every bird an ad for it,
the Sun came out now
we say, meaning
something else went away.
Even fully dressed
we are so naked,
cherish every naked
moment, memory
sunburnt, skin
humming softly to itself.

19 September 2024

Symphony No. 6 in F

1.

Gloom or glow, the garden
gladdens with green vacancy,
gladdens us, we're there
alone, no flowers, trees,
no shrubbery, just us
in the bobble emptiness
of air, the green permission
at our feet. Glad, glad,
we are the garden
and it is us, the space
of walking out the door,
walking out of ourselves
to become more ourselves,
more than ourselves.
Did I just call you a flower?
So be it. Let me.
I am the garden too,
we grow each other,
we bear witness to the light.

2.

Listen to old music,
watch the pilgrims
stepping down the gangplank
into other people's garden,
cautious, greedy for grace,
greedy for green.
Or listen to the big boats now
honking in the channel,
cell phones in their hands
the crew comes home.
Everybody hurries
to the garden. This one,
the given, stolen,
appropriated, don't
count the trees, don't
pick the flowers. Not yet
at least, till you have learned
the special chemistry of each,
atomic structure of
the simplest afternoon.
We see ourselves right there,
the sun always behind us.

3.

Once there was a couple
with a little dog they
carried on the boat
that brought them here.
The dog in her arms
was noisy, sometimes shy
and sometimes wiggling
out of her clutches to run
all around the cabin. As if,
as if, as if it knew too
where we were headed,
the garden everywhere,
can't wait to run around
and only the sea to know
before that other knowing.
Dream with me
what he did
when he ran ashore
and all the questions stopped,
bear with me while
I try to negotiate
the pale green distances
of pure going, and tell me
what was I doing on a boat.

19 September 2024

Symphony No. 7 in D

1.

Wave-forms replicate
thought-forms. Thinking
lashes towards, washes
up upon a thought,
soaks it with surmise
then falls back, rolls back
as if half frightened
of what it has just
learned, known, experienced,
discovered–whatever
thinking thinks it does,
so melodious, the sea.
Do we think better
by the shore? Carl
Sauer called us littoral,
seacoast creatures,
best when our eyes
and ears are washed
by that worldwide
commerce of water and wit.

But it's dawn now,
too bright to read a book.

2.

I call it dawn
but maybe I'm alone.
Calm sea, no rain,
the wind even still asleep.
This is my chance
the eagle thinks
to rule the sky alone,
alone, and no one
hurt or even bothered
by my empery,
my rule of wing,
high notes even
of my sovereign scream
over water over land
and no one harmed–
that is a good country
where all are still asleep
and I am king,
and I can declare
anything at all
the sea brings to mind.

3.

A roll of drums,
a Russian thing
to think we know
what eagles think,
or any other creature
or even the people
across the street,
their house still dark.
Dawn I say, but still
the light does not increase.
That sort of thinking,
sort of day not quite yet,
littoral indeed, always
on the edge of something,
rustling in the surf,
listen hard to hear
what's really there
only here. A little
lighter maybe, triumph,
a man walks up the road.

20 September 2024

Symphony No. 8 in C

1.

All we have to do is
sing along with him,
the shepherd we can't hear,
the shepherd in the hills
of Cappadocia, among the towers
three thousand years ago,
piping to his flock,
sing along with what
we can't hear, not even
his sheep pay much attention
but we need his song
in our breath, lips,
even sintering words
to sounds so that we know,
know and go on browsing
in our intricate world,
each note a blade of grass
to feed us slowly,
feed us
deep.

2.

Then come downhill
and sparkle with the sea,
flutes and bagpipes
and wind whipping the sails
but we stay safe ashore
spending our days as usual
trying to remember.
Slowly, slowly, getting
it right doesn't matter
as much as getting it at all,
the princess sleeps
on the loggia of
her seaside palazzo,
why are we on that
side of the sudden sea?
She stirs in sleep,
her breath a little heavy,
so many decisions
she's had to make, so many
commands to issue, no
wonder she's napping now
and we are far away again,
still trying to catch
a tune some bird

is tweeting sweet
but all we hear
is the Carolina wren,
its single imperious shout.
And then we climb
the hill again
to hide among the towers
where, they say, wise
men used to live alone.

3.

Because lifting
off the earth
makes sense,
Yeats did it in Sligo
and we followed
up his stone steps,
we climbed the cement
tree-trunk steps
up Haussman's artificial hill
over the residue of centuries
and breathed the better for it
but still can't hear
the Anatolian shepherd,
geography and gratitude

and a little girl laughing
as she rides an old ram,
doesn't the fleece tickle,
aren't you Turkish,
why can you hear
that shepherd playing
that we cannot,
even though we
have to go on and on
singing along anyhow?

20 September 2024

Symphony No. 9 in B Minor

1.

Let us suppose that when we die
we persist as voices
in the inmost sky.
Call us echoes, call us ghosts,
the news keeps coming,
as all that we have learned
in this life of wherever,
forever, tumbles from us now
the still-living hear at times
as whispers in their
what should we call it,
soul, mind? Say sky
and make it easy.

2.

Here the priest fell silent,
wrapped his green robe
around him, settled back
on his gilded armchair,
shivered in the cold
temple, and let the chorus

begin their journey,
how loud can wisdom be,
and hope and prayer
and all the things we tend
to hide in music so
they leap out from sound
and we feel what we
are told to feel, a moment
at least of it. But soon
the priest stands up,
the chorus pauses,
breathes easy, leans
against each other's shoulders
and waits for words to stop
and something else comes in.

3.

Sometimes in a cathedral
or mosque or temple
a pigeon flies in, at times
perches in the clerestory
or even nests on a column.
Or a dove. Or a sparrow.
Who are we to decide
what is alive, or choose

what they should do.
Call it a dove, and liken it
to inspiration, or call it
time, fluttering shadows,
look at your watch,
wonder how long
the liturgy will last
or this opera you spent
money and a whole evening
attending, foreign words
shouted in the dim theater,
opera houses are temples too,
his final aria walks
home with you all the way.

4.

But how pleasant
to be outside
fresh air in darkness,
even your partner's
cigarette doesn't spoil it,
air and that sort of silence
only outside knows how to bring.
No more religion, right?
No more other people's music

tonight. Walk slowly,
sidewalks are tools
against anxiety, slow,
think only your own thoughts.
Till you begin to wonder
not for the first time,
not for the last,
who is it who thinks in me?

5.

Walking home
is the purest song,
even a child knows
how to sing it
perfectly. We step
by staring straight ahead
and all around, we
count the trees
and dodge the cars
cats cross our paths
and make us smile,
the bars are open
but their presence
cheers us enough so
we don't have to go in,

onward, this is music
it sings itself, that's
the point of it, somewhere
someone is listening,
someone hears us
everywhere we go.

20 September 2024

Symphony No. 10 in D

1.

Be ordinary as you can
the doctor ordered,
no triremes from Malta
no triumphs on Tiber,
be plain as you can,
holidays are holy days
yes, but every day is holy,
homely, garbage cans
and fences, jury, empty
mailbox, dirt and ditches,
sidewalk swooning
in the Fresno sun—
be ordinary, ordinary,
health is on the way,
meet it at the corner,
lean on the lamp post, wait.

2.

Waited, yes, we did,
in the theater, waited
an hour in the dim,

house-lights down,
waited an hour more
until we began to think
and think that maybe
we were ourselves the play,
our clothes the costumes,
our fears the basic plot.
What are we doing here
and why, we murmur,
but still a little fascinated
by that woman in the row
ahead, the one with auburn hair
and a fur collar I longed
to touch, yes, it and her,
yes, I was there, I'm talking
for myself, what self
I can get a handle on
in this incredibly boring play,
the only show in town.
Wait, wait, there is always
breath, our breath,
breathing is the least
boring action of all.

3.

Sometimes thinking
sounds like zither,
sometimes Gypsies
come strolling up the block,
sometimes I pretend
to speak their language,
sometimes the leaves
start yellowing early
and I try to stop them
falling, I slept then
as if it were a holiday
and no sooner did I wake
when all my friends poured in,
lissome and lovely
and heavy and hard
and who knows the answer
to the question they
for all their love
refuse to ask. Ask
if you love me. Ask
if you're really there.

20 September 2024

Symphony No. 11 in G

1.

Fire escape in lower Manhattan
earthenware flower bowl
full of tiny blue flowers,
forget-me-nots so
it must be spring.
A cat lies on a mat
watching birds, always
pigeons, sometimes
a single cowbird
catches its eye, a little wind
so the two-winged curtain
in the window flutters
and flutters, inviting
our gaze. There floats
the problem. Our eyes
drawn to the curtain
as cat's to the birds.
He knows enough not to
jump at them, knows
he's three stories above
a hard sidewalk. What

do we know as we stare
fascinated at the curtain?
Who is in there, what
are they doing? Aged,
adolescent, guy
chomping a Danish
before work, a woman?
A woman? We know nothing,
ya nichevo ne znayu
we quote from Russian class, sounds like music,
means I know nothing,
the cat has more chance
of catching an owl
than we have, alright, than
I have of knowing
who moves or is still
behind the trembling cotton.
The image conceals
what we have come to see.

2.

Accident used to mean
anything that happens,
anything not part of essence,
not sketched out

in the original design.
Accident could mean
hearing a violin playing
as you walk in the woods,
or finding a nickel on the tin
table, sidewalk café, tip
so meager the waiter
does not deign to pick it up,
remember coins? Never mind,
go, back to the woods,
what was that music?
Bach-ish...did you know
Bach and Handel were
born in the same year?
Was that an accident,
or an island in the ocean?
Or pigeon droppings
on a lawyer's shoulder,
white splotch on his blue
suit, so many birds
downtown these days.
I think it's part of the design.

3.

Now be noble, now be nice,
stop thinking about
the fabulous woman
in her imagined kitchen,
leave her to her morning chai
or is it afternoon already,
the pastoral feeling
even downtown can get
as the sun slopes towards Jersey.
Leave her safe in your ignorance.
There's a nice coffee house
down the block, friendly
faces all around you
as you drink your cappuccino.

4.

But to tell us all the truth
it was the woods I really wanted,
with or without Vivaldi
or whoever, even without
Maria Callas I first heard
in Café Cino on Cornelia,
cities don't leave you
when you leave them,

they still map out
secret places in the soul,
Beethoven or Bushwick
come with you, like
Liszt's dozen grand pianos
on his way to the Sultan,
wait, I'm getting lost in music,
it's the woods I want
to be lost in, the endless
conversation of the trees,
no fiddles, no flute,
a crow call says enough,
I will be quiet now a while,
just be a part of the design.

22 September 2024

Symphony No. 12 in E

1.

Born again, the wheel
still spinning,
commitments ripening
on every side,
fox in the fern brake,
call this music,
ambassadors assembled
the treaty signed
blank piece of legal paper
parchment mind
and then the hurt of knowing
the blue dance
we're caught in by looking,
sun over hazel,
ancient scholars gazing
into the pool
to know what moves
and what stands still,
goldfinch collides
gently with the kitchen window
flits away unharmed

may all our meetings be so we can
name that thing
you see swimming so deep.

2.

The queen slipped into her robe,
faux-fur for she believed
in life, scarlet satin, lifts a phone,
thinks better of it,
drinks her tea.
The phone rings, no
doubt disappointed at neglect.
She does not answer.
The calendar is news enough.
O softly softly say her story,
she wasn't always silent
but when you rule the world
it does all your talking for you.
She remembers her father
saying something like that
back in the days when he
would still answer the phone.

3.

Trying to make light of,
the mood, the matter,
Baroque oboe, you heard her,
the girl in the tee-shirt
running through the thicket
humming deeper than
you expect a girl to hum,
she saw the fox too,
the oboe she was remembering,
eluded her tessitura,
I hurried at an angle
past her politely, it all
is music, isn't it,
no room for silence,
wake up each day
in a new religion,
last note on the bassoon.

22 September 2024

Symphony No. 13 in F

1.

At the stone chess tables
in Washington Square
the old men play, some
for fun and some for money,
plus a cunning younger
Slav coining cash from them
by his midgame skills.
One of the men has a big
shaggy black dog
asleep at his feet.
This is yesterday,
this is leaves faintly
amber toppling from trees.
Do you think chess is fun,
and what about dogs,
who are they in all this,
so patient in the picture,
their masters in tune with
I suppose their breathing.
And chess, horsehead,
bishop's mitre, who am I

fooling when I nudge
a queen up a diagon
and say Hah! to my playmate?
And why are Russians
so good at chess, is it
they have more castles?
Are we all just pawns?

2.

But at the fountain
it's mostly young,
some daring to splash,
some content with vexing
nearby ears with strummed
guitars. Music should be
outlawed, especially because
music at its best is always
against the law, against
the government, I mean,
keeping faith with,
obedient only to, the heart.
Still in summer we hear
the water splash, feeble fountain
but at least it's wet, won't look
like Paris or Rome but

you still can sprinkle it deftly
at a girl and make her
frown with a hint of a smile.
People who live in cities
have to take nature
into their own hands.
Can't leave it all to the dog.

3.

Not far west
the subway rolls
(play it on
the slide trombone)
and past that the streets
run queer-cut to the river
itself an arm of the sea,
our lordly estuary.
Now you know. Kids
play basketball on the corner—
someday a magic moment
comes when the ball
drops through the hoop
and disappears, the boys
go home and read
whatever books the magic

world permits, ancient
scripture, Talmud,
Missal, Sherlock Holmes–
all to make sure the ball
is gone. Toys kill truth.
I keep a keyboard
hidden in my undershirt,
all my breaths and movements
make it keep typing
all day long. Bedtime
I take it out, lay it chastely
beside my pillow, so all
night long I can dream
the urgent text it scribed.
Tomorrow I'll tell you what I said.

22 September 2024

Symphony No. 14 in B

1.

Sun over Vineyard
dogs at the door,
one Sun, two of them,
small brown siblings
evidence of strangers
in the neighborhood, hmm...
One sea under one sky,
one hand held mine
as we got back to sleep
just before dawn. One day,
two dawns, how many any
does it take to make one?
The Sun a hydrophone
artist making one
sea sing so many songs.
Your hand at dawn
felt so loving in mine.

2.

Stop counting, neighbor.
The dogs are gone,

the light increases,
the old religion stays new,
down where the yachts live
they sing a song
made up just to give
us something to remember.
What else is music for?
the captain asks
then we sing louder
to tell him. Theme
slithers forward through sound,
the words hardly matter
though they're our only matter.
What are they saying now?
The Sun comes up every day
but we can't always see it–
whose fault is that?
Whose dogs navigate the deck?
O lovely organ tones
of gentle aimless questions,
twilight in an empty church.

3.

Take everything that happens
and sign your name to it.

The teacher was emphatic,
lay claim to everything,
every disease a declaration,
each stumble an Olympic feat.
Wealth management!
Street music in autumn,
Calabrian neighborhood,
statues cast shadows too,
their shadows move
though they stand still,
learn, learn, the teacher
screamed, sign the treaty,
my life is in your hands!
We soothed the man
by leaving with a smile,
and took the subway home.
Or was that our true home,
all going, all underground?

4.

The soldiers roused
buzzed awake by drones
slipping through dawn,
ours or theirs no way
of telling till too late.

I switched the channel
and watched surfers
negotiate Point Lobos.
Noise is always the enemy,
I think they come there
half-naked to be targeted
by the noise of waves
fisting its way against the shore.
O why not just for once
stay home, endure
the ticking of the toaster,
the hum of our new
microwave and O
dear God the wind outside?

23 September 2024

Symphony No. 15 in B Flat

1.

Hawk's house our habitat,
we fell from sky
and share and share
and the wind is the same
and every minute is
a feather in the flight of time,
hawk hovers, we linger.
Put on sunglasses
when you check your watch.
Numbers have sharp edges,
bird beak and talons
and wait for the claw.
Alertness is the widest country,
the savannas of vision
you expect in your
landscape, a bird looks down,
on the widest country,
sea to sea and who knows
how deep the caverns,
I do not dare to look.

2.

But once I was a little boy
and went beneath the ground.
Cold down there, and wet,
wet walls and a stream
running north as if it knew,
knew what I'm still
trying to find out, where
is anything, where
should everything be?
I still feel the wet stone walls
as if anything we touch
becomes part of us.
Ask your lovers how much
of them is you.

3.

Prairie easy, prairie rest,
wind combs the cornfield,
walk home after school,
a hill is something over there,
something that happens
to the horizon but we,
me, all the me's, are at peace.
Our life is a tabletop

maybe, a place to dance,
a hand resting on the lawn,
a dozen at noon, a shade
suddenly rolls up,
there we are, exposed
as we really are, alive,
accurate only to the moment,
it's all one country, one kitchen,
calendar flapping on the door,
president on the P.O. wall
one baptism, one battle,
my hand in your pocket,
forgive me for the truth.

4.

Hespera men én

Then it was night.
The Athenians
folded their tablets
and tried to sleep.
They knew the war
was on the way,
it always is, they mumbled
their prayers and slept.

Think of dishes drying
by the sink, think
of lions asleep on the veldt,
think of mirrors
that learn to talk,
emeralds and shooting stars,
every word is a cry for help
so hope the sky hears—
nothing else is still awake.

23 September 2024

Symphony No. 16 in A Minor

1.

Lay the lesson down
at the teacher's feet,
oak or alder,
gentle autumn day
anxious with answers
for us, we need them,
we're a main part
of their lesson plan,
the trees, the world-wide
university, study tree sap
from Zanzibar, you can hear
strange languages
as someone walks by
perfumed therewith,
words of the trees
not always apples,
some are hidden deep
in grain, remember
that woman who slipped
past us in patchouli,
was it California?

But why do we need
to remember, the sycamore-
maples are right outside,
one even shielding
our little patio,
too chilly to sit out
there this morning
later we'll sit out a while
and read the lesson
even their shadows leave.

2.

Everything lasts longer
when you listen,
have you noticed?
Some rabbis think
the world is still slowly
listening to the first word.
But then the clash
of cymbals says Now now
now, as if there never
was another time and we're
still waiting for the word.
Choose your religion,
choose your truth.

Every leaf of every
tree is a page torn
from a sutra you have to find
or dream a summation of—
doze now, as the music calms.

3.

Or leap up
like Bruckner
or be animal,
noble or nimble,
shout to wake yourself,
you're the only one
this selfish world requires,
workmen hammering outside,
horses clopping through Vienna
O come back to California,
that girl up Topanga Canyon,
where has the Sun gone
while you were sleeping?
There are some sounds
that feel like scents,
our nervous system
is a busy marketplace
in Jericho three thousand

years ago busy being now,
rustle of silk, sparrows
or are they shadows,
you can almost recognize
the odor what comes
along on the wind,
but never name it
even if you could,
no trees in the desert
but they're all
safe inside you.

24 September 2024

Symphony No. 17 in A#

1.

The famous pianist
sat on his terrace
finger-tapping
on his glass-topped table
to the rhythm of the old
Cork come-all-ye tangle-fish
tangle-fish, who loops the heart?
Nice to hear them, him,
cheery chat of rapped-on
glass, occasional click
of fingernail, but what
is music for? Or afternoons?
And what kind of fish
could the Irish mean,
amphimacer, amphimacer
who does what to whom?
But I liked hearing him play,
play in the true sense
of the word, and I thought
about a big blackfish
six fathoms down, hungering

among the rocks down there,
feeding on lobster and crab.
Nice to sit here thinking,
hearing him tinkle away,
lucky to know him, lucky
to sit here, music
is like an afternoon
compared to the stricter
arts, music lets you rest
watching without much anxiety
sun slip down to the same sea.

2.

Then he stopped fingering,
looked at me boldly,
What are you thinking?
he demanded of me,
so I sighed and I tried
to deliver. He seemed
annoyed, interrupted me,
music is the strictest art,
the only one that tells you
when you're wrong,
the only one that yanks you
to your feet or makes you grab

somebody and start to dance,
makes you cry when
you're not even sad.
Basta, basta, I yelped,
you've made your point,
it's because you played
only the rhythm and left
out the tune, what could I do
but improvise? He calmed,
rang a little bell, his valet
brought out two cups of chai.

3.

But I went on swimming
down there in the sea
his fingers and my mind
had married to create,
down there with the tautog,
sometimes surfacing
to watch the hermit crab
leave her eggs on the beach
for her several husbands
to make love to in their way,
O it's all love song, even
the worst of it, baroque

boredom, twelve-tone twaddle.
And then I saw him
looking angry at me again
as if he read my mind.
Only then did I remember
what music does, is for,
means. Music reads the mind.

25 September 2024

Symphony No. 18 in D Minor

1.

Under Antarctic ice
is waiting
land low, a groan
of green maybe
centuries to come
we fear the sea
our mother rising
to take us back in
when the snow melts
and then the ice goes
and coastlines shrink
and we blame ourselves,
we always do, nobody else,
to pin the fault on,
Spicer said "my
vocabulary
did this to me,"
ours too, carbon,
alcohol, gas and coal.

2.

So we set up windmills
to borrow air,
and spread mirrors
on our meadows
to steal the light—
or borrow it, or is it
ours to start with,
free gift of the sun,
our other mother?
It took more than one
womb to make a world?

3.

So arid this music
so easy to understand.
Word chop and hand clap
as if we were Shakers
or something, folkish
as knitting, wise
as a schoolhouse
shuttered for summer,
no, more than that,
whistle my wisdom
in bland music,

no hint of color, wheedle
until you look up
from your crossword
and say Thanks
for the hint,
put down the paper,
go out and pat the white dog.

4.

There, is that more like music,
is that why you piled
into this chilly auditorium
to listen to what
someone else was thinking,
thinking out loud
until you closed your eyes
and loved it, or wished
you were back home
and could turn on the radio
and hear something
that finally made sense?

26 September 2024

Symphony No. 19 in E flat

1.

Talisman, tell us a tale,
the one you wear
around the neck
of that drowsy soldier
holding his head
with his hands, fingers
over his tired eyes,
why is he so sad,
and this piece of silver
you are, tinkling a little
as he sighs, as you clink
against his army badge,
where do you come from,
who gave it to him,
what do you mean?
But from the embers
of the dying fire
in the fireplace a voice
hisses What does anything mean?
How dare you asssssssssssk?

2.

Next morning I asked him
directly, he smiled
and said his girl
had given it to him
to keep him safe,
she was pure Roma
and knew about such things,
and his colonel let him
wear it on a ribbon,
teased him a little
but obviously took
all that Gypsy stuff
seriously. It kept him
safe in battle, and one thing
the others noticed
was how birds would gather
around him whenever
we rested out there
where birds love
and women understand.

3.

O forget the war,
recall the birds,

forget the lovers even
and remember
only the silver
twinkling on his chest,
forget the color even
but recall the light,
glint, gleam, glimmer,
call it what you like.
It comes from the East
the way the Roma do.

4.

We needed those drumrolls
those bugles to wake us
from being awake
and work a miracle
of time inside time
turned inside out,
a friend called it
remembering the future
and she knew,
she had been reading books
for two and a half thousand years
and could smell
what is to come.

The soldier packed up
his gear and left the inn,
the war is over, he smiled
at me as if we had
actually talked.
But we had shared the same fire.

26 September 2024

Symphony No. 20 in B Minor

1.

The monks in their red robes
go out to the near hills
and settle down here and there
pretending to be stones
so the stones of the hillside,
sandstone and shale and gneiss,
begin to talk to them
feeling safe with their kin—
though they know
the monks are pretending
but that kind of pretense
is good for the soul
and food for the rock, too.
And so they talk on and on
and the monks listen,
a few of them even daring
to say a word or two back.
All afternoon—the best time—
the conversations continue
till at dusk, the monks
hungry now but also

satisfied, hurry home for supper.
Then the hard work begins,
writing down, each monk alone,
what they have heard
during the sun time of the day.
Dozen monks dozen manuscripts.

2.

But O what do they say?
I read one once
and spent the night at it,
weeping and laughing
and finally understanding
something I never knew
before, something about
the nature of time, be easy,
don't worry, time is only
the musculature of space,
it took me all these years
to get where I am,
and you where you are,
even though there seems to be
only a yard of carpeting
between where I'm sitting
and where you stand

by the window, watching
the sparrows spend
their precious time aloft.

3.

Then it all seems off,
my monk got it wrong,
stone envies our mobility,
we envy its gravity,
its unforgetting, its
changelessness through
our sense of time.
Where would music be
if time were space?
Are we in Leipzig
whenever we hear Bach,
are we in Uttar Pradesh
hearing Saraswati's wise
fingers on her long strings?

4.

And sometimes I feel just dumb,
all the words and all the stones
slip away and the gray sky
tells me to wait, wait and pray,

or wait and say nothing
till it says itself in me.
Is the sky my stone
making a monk of me?
Once I was a pirate
and had no ship,
an aviator then
without a plane,
and now I am a speaker
without a word,
no strings on my harp.
Stone, stone, sing me instead.

26 September 2024

Symphony No. 21 in D

1.

For all the rolling of the green
the roiling of the sea
boiled into storm of sky
to bruise the land,
storm after storm
we do most of us survive,
safe in the clamshell of hope
we wear around our minds.
Strong sunlight
on the sea,
raindrops on
the window screen.
Take comfort
where you can,
the hurricane is
in you too–
can we mood
this world to peace?

2.

Music investigates
the spaces between.
Between of course
what happens and what
could happen. What else
could love songs be up to,
or organ praises
of the unseen Lord?
Kay's meditation on the Pieta,
English horn and strings
seemed the national anthem
of Between, hope and fear
and love and grief all
caught in the mind.
And willing to endure
themselves, the heroic
endurance of what we feel.

3.

These words though
are far from the wind,
is a man cheating if he says
anything at all about
what he himself is not

experiencing, just hears
about, reads about?
What do I know about Moses,
what do I know about the moon?
O memory, that sandbag
on the mind, to weigh it down
inside its own experience,
keep it dry from really
understanding, drenched
by all that comes now.

4.

Blame me with snare drum,
apologize with bassoon—
there, the opposites tangle
and wake me from thinking
into this other countryside
half-weather half-wonder—
are we there yet
the child asks
and nobody knows,
how could they,
the sun still shining?

27 September 2024

Symphony No. 22 in C

1.

Dawn do it.
The long
diagon of cloud
leans over the island,
the other island.
The other,
we are here
for the other,
the Sun and the sea are
and we are of their
conspiracy, their breaths
breathing together
for the other,
and from all the murmur
a quiet voice
in a mountain accent
but perfectly clear
looked out over the sea
and said Be simple,
we are for the other.

2.

Easy to think
harder to do.
Doing is the problem
child of thinking.
Rattle of bamboo
as you struggle
through thickets,
slosh of mud on my feet
as I hurry to her house,
his house, your house
near Othertown in Otherland
just to bring you this flower,
daisy sort of, biggish,
white and yellow
like this white sky
with you know what,
and here it is,
lodged on your porch
too early to knock
on any door and say
here is your flower.
But here is your flower.

3.

I was born on an island
you were born on mainland.
You grew up on island,
I left, never went back again.
We have much to teach
each other, other,
like violin and cello
or we'd never be complete.
Even in our rustic Otherville
music needs to be loud,
complex, leave simplicity
to the clouds, those
affable muscular
breasts in the sky
we sometimes get
to drink from, the rain
is not only for flowers,
no, that's just silly,
we all are flowers too.

28 September 2024

Symphony No. 23 in F Minor

1.

Once on Long Island
I saw a whale
on display in a pool,
big enough but
not the biggest kind,
black and glistening.
I reached out far
as I could and stroked
his smooth tough hide,
then he spurted a plume
of water from his spout
and some of it caught me,
sleeve and shoulder,
forehead and glasses
what a blessing, wet
kiss of a whale, this must be
my baptism by the sea.

2.

So little makes liberty,
so little makes love.

We live by trifles
and build with them
great monuments
of notice and attentions
paid. A theory
is more valuable
than any pyramid,
tell that to the desert
some blue night
and watch the stars agree.
Come build with me
each sand grain says,
leave the rocks undisturbed
to their millennial
investigations and play
with little, make it big.
Then I remember the whale
like a tune from childhood
long forgotten, then,
then the sea. And I recall
being splashed by it–
and think it made me me.

3.

Some music has to be small,
small and fast,
like a sparrow
flashing past your window.
The more birds,
other birds, again
and again, always
the same window,
same song,
so many tiny pieces
to be heard, seen,
so many flashes, seafoam
drenching the eager silence.

30 September 2024

Symphony No. 24 in G

1.

Slide, slide,
across the street
on snow or Luna Park,
wet or dry,
sled or grass,
the word, the slide,
the swift movement
with no moving, slide,
to be an object only,
thingly streaking
or sluggisher downhill,
sled or slip,
slide on slippery,
downhill yowling
and be sailing
sea-free and dry,
almost dry,
doing nothing,
doing nothing but going!
Going fast and always here!
The slide, I said the slide.

2.

Mothers worry
slow and solemn
about such doings,
are they right?
Right to hope a kid
doesn't learn to expect
everything to come his way
or he can go get it
just by lying on his back
and looking at the sky
or at the playmates
all around applauding
his sassy giggly descent.
Rise up, rascal,
do some work
to get what you
must learn to want!
she rants, then she
remembers how he
got here in the first place
because she lay down
on her back one fine day
and let it all begin,
she let the world happen

that slow
nine month slide.

3.

Too much moralizing
here, forgive the slack,
too few pictures.
Here's one: Venezuelans
at the fishing dock
scooping up carp
with long-handled nets.
People plus fish
plus river plus tool.
What more can
any workday want,
a parking space?
Way above the fisher folk
a grassy slope for all
to tumble down,
big riverbank rocks
to keep our eternal
slider from the river.
The slider! That's who's
been whee!-ing
his way, her way, our way,

how can I tell,
they're all going
too fast, going faster,
down, they live
on an angle that finally
mates with earth,
faster, the glory of it,
to go and go and not be gone.

2 October 2024

About the Author

Robert Kelly was born in 1935 in Brooklyn, and lived mostly on the south shore. He studied at CCNY and Columbia. In 1961, his first book of poetry *Armed Descent*, was published. In the same year, he began six decades of teaching at Bard College, where he taught literature and writing until 2023. Kelly's extensive and influential body of published work includes most recently, *Linden Word, Earish*, (homeophonic translations of Celan) and *Listening Through*. He lives in the Hudson Valley with his wife, the celebrated French translator Charlotte Mandell.